More Praise for *Luminous Body, Glittering Ash*

"I was falling in love with the world, and everything in the world was dying," writes C.W. Emerson in *Luminous Body, Glittering Ash*. A reader will be drawn in by the narrator's compelling voice in this lyric narrative that captures a moment in history when a man caretakes the lives of those dearest to him, even in the midst of a pandemic, and though he might hope to save them all, it is not within his hands to hold them.

—Sandra Alcosser, author of
A Fish to Feed All Hunger and *Except by Nature*

This is a poignant, fine-wrought book of poise and lamentation—by turns, erotic, austere, and lyrical—with a keen attention to natural beauty. Its centerpiece poems, "The Impossible Time" and "Coldwater Canyon Suite," convey the saga of what it meant to be young, gallant, and compassless in the shocking early years of the AIDS epidemic. Because that was my experience as well, reading C.W. Emerson's *Luminous Body, Glittering Ash* made for a powerful aide-mémoire of that daunting, heartbreaking era. Emerson's intrepid survivor's task, his elegiac portraiture and vivid witness pierce us out of necessity.

—Cyrus Cassells, 2021 Poet Laureate of Texas
and author of *The World That the Shooter Left Us*

The radiant from which *Luminous Body, Glittering Ash* emanates is the body's own perishable luminosity, these poems the lyric record of the body's trajectory as a falling star—meteoric, brief—during the height of the AIDS pandemic. Like those meteors, Emerson convinces us, our transits leave a crypto-crystalline gleam, yet the heart, to be safe, leaves the body, turns invisible, but continues to throw sparks long after it stops. Emerson's deftly trenchant

poems never succumb to bathos but pinpoint the *l'heure exquise* of our fleeting existence and name it, a quality that destines this collection to become a classic in league with Thom Gunn's *The Man with Night Sweats*.
—Lise Goett, author of *Leprosarium*

I don't know what to say about C.W. Emerson's poems except that they break my heart over and over again, and then again, and in that breakage, there's something luminous, always—as if your ability to be broken, in itself, makes us ever more human, ever more broken, ever more human. These poems are brave and beautiful, crystal clear, and deeply mysterious, they embody the sensual and the sacred, without contradiction, without apology. I'm grateful to have them to read and to remind me what it is to be fully alive.
—Cecilia Woloch, author of *Tsigan: The Gypsy Poem*

LUMINOUS BODY, GLITTERING ASH

LUMINOUS BODY, GLITTERING ASH

C.W. Emerson

World Enough
Writers

Copyright © 2025 C.W. Emerson
All rights reserved.

No part of this publication may be reproduced, distributed, or transmitted in any form or by any means whatsoever without written permission from the publisher, except in the case of brief excerpts for critical reviews and articles. All inquiries should be addressed to World Enough Writers.

Poetry
ISBN 978-1-937797-10-2

Cover art: *Untitled* (Pool, 2025) by Salomon Huerta
oil on canvas, 70" x 50"
photographed by Pablo Aguilar

Author photo: Rand Larson

Book design: Tonya Namura,
using Minion Pro (text) and Avenir Next (display)

World Enough Writers, an imprint of Concrete Wolf Poetry Series, is dedicated to publishing poetry collections and anthologies of global relevance and importance.

World Enough Writers
c/o Concrete Wolf
PO Box 2220
Newport, OR 97365-0163

WorldEnoughWriters@gmail.com

https://WorldEnoughWriters.com

For Daniel, and our light-bearing comrades:

we familial, we mundane,
we flaming profane,
we divine.

CONTENTS

I. LUMINOUS BODY

"Didn't I stand there once…"	5
Time Travels of the Older American Poet	6
The Gardener	7
Body	9
Safe	10
Pinehurst, 2014 / (My Father to His Wife)	12
The Impossible Time	14
Coldwater Canyon Suite	16
Morning Poem	31
To G, Late November, Six Weeks Married	32
Love & Bone	33
Request	34

II. ASH

"What do they know…"	39
Sandstorm	40
Joe	41
Prayer	45
Neighborhood Watch	46
Illuminé	50
The Jenkins Boy	51
Darkling	53
Easter Portrait, 1964 / (Father to Son)	55
My Father's Death	57

The Family Line	60
What Was Promised	62
Miguel	63
Afterword	65
Acknowledgments	67
Gratitude	69
About the Author	71

LUMINOUS BODY, GLITTERING ASH

I want to be the grieving gardener
of the earth you fill and fertilize,
my dearest friend, so soon....

Across the stubble of the dead I walk
uncomforted, leaving my heart behind,
going about my business.

>   —Miguel Hernández, "Elegy for Ramón Sijé"
>   trans. Edwin Honig (from *The Unending
>   Lightning*, 1990)

>   Rain lost brothers.
>   Let joy reunite itself with itself.
>   The soul of the sky, fill it with rain.
>   Rain the plumage of the forgotten.
>   This simple but necessary instruction:
>   Undress the sky.
>   Rain the dead.

>   —Mitchell Untch, "Rainsong"

I. LUMINOUS BODY

Didn't I stand there once,
nineteen, loose-limbed,

dripping water onto the catwalk
above the motel pool?

And weren't we luminous then?—
our bodies glistening,

pale as the slice of winter moon
that hung in a Vegas sky.

Wasn't there a door, a threshold,
one simple, white-walled room?

You'd have become
bobcat, eucalyptus, salt cedar,
my love—

had you lived a little longer.

TIME TRAVELS OF THE OLDER AMERICAN POET

Today, coming home from an exhibition,
    The Surrealistic Adventures of Women Artists,
        I tripped and fell into a hole of sky,

tumbled up, and landed
        at the Locke Insulator Company,
Victor, New York, circa 1903.

I saw my grandfather, five years old,
    held in the arms of my great-uncle Pete,
        with their father in his basement laboratory,

mixing silica, filling beakers, stealing heat
        from great-grandmother's oven
long past a decent hour of the night.

Great-grandfather Locke and Sons
    molded their molten glass
        into green and purple domes—

thick, smooth, helmet-headed—
        to perch atop telephone poles
and line the railroads of a nation newly on the move.

These Irish, these unschooled,
    these pre-autistic geniuses:

my heart is linked to their hearts
    by something like the cord
        that links *The Two Fridas*,

both sitting earthbound, politely, in chairs,
        their glistening aortas exposed.

THE GARDENER

Ismael stands by the old back gate,
come to prune roses
        where no roses grow,

only cottonwood and cactus
pushing through sand,

tender agave, brittle ocotillo,
the rutted yucca he fought
        so hard to save
from last year's drought.

        *

I think of James, my grandfather,
and his miniature orange trees—

the five years they took to bloom
in the big bay window
        on Catherine Street,

how he sketched, then painted
his tropical scenes
        from memory—
the Cuban coast, the Florida Keys—

and marked each day
in red-lined journals,
year after snowbound year.

        *

Ismael stands
on the cracked clay tiles,
morning gone to noontime blaze,

straw hat
        tilted down
to hold him in its shadow,

a waxed-paper parcel
in his hands:

three soft figs,
        still warm from the tree.

BODY

The body is a map
of what befalls it—

both a map and
the territory it signifies.

Its borders are drawn
on bruised and sutured flesh.

    *

My body is a map
of lake and woodlands,

white with winter,
umber in autumn,

multiple the dreams
by which it is riven.

    *

This is the dream
it is dreaming now:

someone is singing
a lamentation

while the body melts
in the sun's fierce rays.

SAFE

The wind
cuffs the snow
to the side of the road
and leaves it standing

pillow-thick under streetlights,
along the balustrades,
nesting in the bare arms
of trees, like sleeves.

This house would be
a good house
for the winter
with its wide-plank floors

and its joists that meet
at sharp right angles.

In this house,
my brother holds me down,
my face pressed against
the plank's rough grain—

but then, unscathed,
set free by summer,

I throw the old, black
       screen door open
              and let the world
come flying in:

bees from hives,
            the lint of leaves—

webs that spin themselves into gold
float in on the morning haze.

*

In winter, asbestos warms the house.
Honey's amber hides in the comb.

This is how I have come to be
an old brick wall half standing

> in a field
> by a road
> in the snow.

PINEHURST, 2014 / (MY FATHER TO HIS WIFE)

It was in the evening, after supper.

We were discussing love and order,
compromise and its place in our lives

when I tipped from my chair like an egg
tumbling from its nest,
gracelessly, onto the ground.

*

How strange to lose the use of arms
that once effortlessly

stacked wheat, raised sheets
of salvage metal overhead—

to have no feeling left in hands
that once caressed your hands, your arms;

arms you raised so often
between me and the intruding world.

But now, who will keep your secrets
and tend to the crop
we left half-harvested in the field?

*

When I walk out to where the combine
sits silent in its rust, and stand

with the snow packed deep
in the tread of my boots, and listen,

all that I hear
is the faintest of sounds:

a whisper of breath,
                a rattle of bone,
a skittering leaf on a frozen pond—

the body falling apart.

                *

I look out over the acres and days
through the eyes in an old man's face.

The light has changed.
It's a different light,

as though an errant star
has cracked the horizon,

bled the world
of color and hue,

casting me into unexpected night.

THE IMPOSSIBLE TIME

I was falling in love with the world, and everything in the world was dying.

There was no end to what threatened us. I sheltered under leaves, in the dark humus. I waited for it to be over, but it was never over. There would be no future, so we made no plans.

Still, the air had a sweetness and tang; we were young, the lines of our bodies light and lithe, the night air filled with valley jasmine, with smoke from deep in the Tenderloin, with traces of champagne wafting over Brooklyn's snow-clad streets.

That winter, our breath misted the windows of my old Chevy, your new coupe. I was in love with the thought of you. But you were already gone.

*

The leaves and the bodies kept falling around me. I tracked the snowpack as it melted, focused my gaze on the ground below—or did it happen in another way entirely?—in a time of such impossibilities, what exactly is the truth? A narrator soaked in hardscrabble gin, a bulletproof screen that kicks our bullets back at us.

It happened in broken nights littered with fever and sweat-soaked sheets that signaled our imminent demise. There was no escaping death's widening presence. But even so, we would not die.

*

For years I floated above the carnage, then finally rejoined the herd of the living—cleaned out closets, made arrangements, moved through the necessary days. The faces and place-names bent and merged into something that felt like safety. I shadowed the plague from seaboard to seaboard, marched up Fifth Avenue flanked by stars and suffragettes, slunk down Sunset Boulevard with wreckage like me from the streets and alleys.

*

One morning, I woke to a clear sky flocked with white, a dusting of feathers over the Hudson Valley. I prayed that something of our kind would find its way into time's pleats and waves—our grace and beauty, the way we defied expectations of weakness—that despite our decimation, we would endure.

This was how life came back to me, afterward—the way light filters through bamboo shades, insinuates itself, then disperses the night. The planets in their new configurations, a subtle shifting of the elements. Time, its planes like sheets of glass: sharp, translucent, slicing the air.

COLDWATER CANYON SUITE

i. Off Coldwater Canyon, 1982

I was nineteen
when I stepped off the plane
                that had carried me
from Rochester to LA,

away from my father's pronouncements
of what made a man a man,
a life worth living—

just beyond baggage claim
and the hiss
of the electric doors,
                that first blast
of carbon-fueled, dream-filled air

melted the frosted past, quelled
my rising panic, rearranged
the way light fell forever.

                *

I don't remember driving
to North Hollywood that first morning;
but just off Coldwater Canyon
I discovered a place called the Riverton Arms—

apartments linked
by manicured walkways, artfully lit—
which seemed, to me,
                the height of refinement—

a magical compound,
where men loved men and fountains flowed,
and greens exploded into fire-blossom;

where scents of pine and rosemary
mingled and baked in the slow valley days,
and ambient freeway
                white noise lullabies
sang us into morning's smog-soaked light.

        *

Little Sam lived with Roberto,
            and Big Sam with Bob
in a haze of good taste and Italian cologne.

Big Sam wore his moustache
thick and lush,
exactly like the Marlboro Man.

Roberto was covered
with tattoos and piercings,
a pirate on the prowl.

Bob could have been a model for *Colt*,
with his feathered hair and chiseled jaw.

And Little Sam's smile
            was unabashed joy—
a boy from the streets of East LA,
sheltered by lindens and sycamores
lining both sides of Riverton Drive.

I took a studio in the back,
furnished the place with one twin bed,
microphones, cables, electric piano—

spent my days composing songs,
making demos on a two-track reel-to-reel,

imagined them on the radio,
my name rising high on the *Billboard* charts.

For now, my music
seeped through walls
                and flowed over walkways,
letting neighbors know I was home.

         *

Nights and weekends
I worked at the Hayloft
               up on the Boulevard
for minimum wage, plus tips and beer,

serving drinks
to the exquisite sweat-slicked men
               sliding up to the bar
straight off the dance floor.

They traveled in packs, these golden ones,
and came for the reasons
               they'd always come:
to revel, to dream,
to dance away the night—

to see their own reflections
               glitter and gleam
under the blaze of the dance floor lights.

After hours, men would embrace
in darkened corners of the bar,

drinking shots, making toasts
to hopes and ambitions
long forgotten by morning.

      *

For two years, I hustled drinks;
every night, shirtless dancers
swayed to the beat.

One morning in early winter,
upon the scrim of muscle and rib—

    skin that had always been smooth, unblemished—

there, on the naked back of a dancer,
the faintest trace of lavender arose.

When torsos flowered
with fields of purple lesions,
the dancers cleared the dance floor,
           whispered goodbye
to their carefully imagined futures:

to the big house
           in the Hollywood Hills
with the perfect companion,

to the good job
with good insurance
they wouldn't live long enough to use.

      *

The men at the Riverton Arms
                grew fragile, weary,
holding on to old grudges
as they nursed one another—

more companions
than fervent lovers.

Big Sam made plans to leave LA,
headed for the vast Northwest.

Roberto's legs would buckle
every time he tried to leave his bed.

                *

Roberto and Little Sam
had bedrooms that adjoined;
I seemed to be always
                with one or the other
all that winter and into the spring,

doling out medications,
making up beds for visiting family,

walking alone in the April rain
to Henry's Tacos
                for take-out burritos
in grease-soaked paper bags.

And every afternoon,
once the boys were asleep,
Bob and I would steal away,
out to my old Impala—

with the ragtop down
                and the radio cranked,
we'd haul ass the length of the 101,

stopping to check on our bedridden friends:
delivering meals they would rarely eat,
changing the dampened linens,

checking for rashes, fever spikes,
and touching them—

                always, we touched them—

we'd rub their calloused feet,
hold withered hands

gone cold, so often,
                in the afternoon heat.

                *

One sweltering August morning
in a bare-bones church in Eagle Rock,
just northeast of downtown LA,

Bob and I laid Little Sam to rest
in a simple wooden box.

In my pocket, a tiny keepsake urn—
a tablespoon of Roberto's ashes.

Little Sam had been twenty,
younger than I was.

His family was gathered
at the front of the church
where he lay, serene,
                in an open casket—

his father, drunk, as always,
his mother numb,
                her expression blank.

His teenage brothers, Peter and Paul,
trouble in matching leather jackets,

and sister, Amelia,
elegant in black silk crepe,
a single strand of pearls.

The Catholic Mass droned on and on.

I handed the urn to Amelia.
She would sprinkle the ashes
        on her brother's coffin,
later, graveside at Forest Lawn.

I left before the final prayers,
gave no condolences,
              said no goodbyes.

I walked outside to my red Impala,
drove east along the 134
with no destination in mind.

There was no one
who needed attending to,

no reason not to drive on.

ii.   Aftermath, 1985

To a man, they were gone,
my brothers-in-arms,
my lovers, my friends—

    massacred is not too strong a word—

first Rick and Roger,
            then Paco, Danny;

Jason, who had died alone—
he lay dead in the house
        on his Chatsworth ranch
two full days before anyone knew.

Little Sam was the last to go.
It seemed to me that a chapter had closed.

It was time to be finished
            with grief, self-pity,
time to relinquish my rosary of ashes—

time for my life to be something more
than an endless novena,
            a desperate prayer.

God wasn't listening anyway.

I was twenty-two and already old.

      *

I'd spent three years at the Riverton Arms,

       —that dreamlike place,
       set apart from the world,

       redolent with the scent of wild herbs
       and cultivated flowers.

Day after day,
I would drink in that magical Western light,
breathe the smog that burnished it,

forgive the city
            a hundred times over
its indifference
to my starstruck dreams.

But that seemed a hundred years ago.

      *

Of the men I'd known at the Riverton,
only Bob and I remained—

Bob said he needed distance
now that Little Sam was gone.

I watched as he packed and drove away.

I did the things I needed to do:
emptied cupboards,
           bleached the linens,
plunged my hands into scalding water
laced with ammonia,

trying to scrub away
           the blood, the sorrow.

*

The city's radiance was muted,
the lights on the Boulevard dimmed.

I sat on a barstool at the Hayloft,
observed the swagger of
      my young replacement
as he served me tequila and cold Coronas,
everything *on the house*.

Men were filing into the bar
in smaller groups of two or three;
      actors, models, workaday fellows—

they came from offices, clothing stores,
they tracked in the dust
      of construction sites,
or had crawled out of bed at cocktail time.

Some came alone,
wearing denim, leather,
and cautious, wary smiles;

none of them knew if his latest lover
might be the next to fall.

There were still no explanations,
there was no plan, no protocol.

There was nothing to believe in,
nothing and no one to rally behind—

only a new suspicion of strangers,
the fear of contagion, the downcast eyes—
the abiding signs
              of incipient plague.

       *

Hundreds marched
in New York that summer, 1986.

Thousands were sick
in the desiccated South
and throughout the scorched Midwest.

Hollywood wept,
or pretended to weep—
           even then, it seemed to glisten.

I'd lie awake
with the windows open,
the summer night silent as smoke.

I wanted some reminder of paradise—

a whisper of breeze coming down from the canyon,
a note of jasmine in the evening air.

iii.   Reclamation, 1987

Seven months after Bob packed up
                and left the Riverton Arms,
I moved a few miles up the road
from just off Coldwater Canyon
        to the flats of Van Nuys,

settled into a tiny duplex
lodged in a grove of eucalyptus
tucked away on Valerio Street.

Mornings I'd drive
        along Magnolia Boulevard,
stop for breakfast at Four'n 20 Pies,

go to the nine o'clock AA meeting
for lack of anything better to do.

The coolness of fall was coming on;
autumn was lifting
                the dome of smog
that had covered the valley all summer.

By late September,
my money was dwindling—
but I was well, unlike so many others,
and I could work.

I took a job as a caregiver,
                unafraid of becoming ill
from simple, human contact.

Besides, I knew what the role required;
I'd seen men through their final days.

*

I seemed to know instinctively
how to care for my stricken friends—

what I didn't know
I learned from the hospice workers,
middle-aged women with careworn faces,
men with Mohawks, nose rings,
            and coal-black eyes.

But I wasn't prepared to care for strangers—
their eyes were foreign, suffused with fear,
unsettling, unfamiliar.

Each time I touched their bodies
my own revulsion shamed me,
            and every ministration—

swabbing away their acrid sweat,
soothing their lesions with herbal balms—
            left me drained, exhausted,
as though I were the one in need of care.

In the beating of their weakened hearts
was a hunger, an eagerness to live;

but I stood there at their bedsides—
            frozen, helpless,
lacking the will to go on:

      —for these were not the men I'd loved.

*

After a month, I gave notice,
    went home,
sat alone, outside in the garden.

I'd given no thought to what might come next.
I was too numb to think,
    too beaten down,
fatigued beyond anything I could have imagined.

  I hadn't known a person could be so tired.

I sat among the eucalyptus,
their long, plaited leaves
    perfuming the air
with mint and citronella—

a scent so bracing
it cut straight through the midday heat.

That boy who'd stepped off a plane in LA
was only a distant memory.

I was twenty-four,
and all but convinced
the best part of my life was over.

I'd long since set my music aside—
my own ambitions disappearing
    the day I saw,
on the skin of a friend,
those first purple lesions.

I bought myself a real piano,
a secondhand Baldwin upright;

for the first time
            since the carnage began,
I played again, and composed—

odes to LA, inconsolable city:
to days of blue sky powdered with cloud,
        and nights that blazed
            with klieg lights, jasmine;

love songs to the men we'd lost,
and the ones we had yet to lose—

innocent songs
for the boy I'd been,

psalms
for the heartbroken man I'd become.

I found something like hope
alive in the music,

something like freedom
urging me on.

MORNING POEM

Just as creeks quicken
and shadows disperse,

so the ashes in the urn
are only my dark imaginings.

I watch you
lift yourself from the bed
when you don't know I'm watching.

TO G, LATE NOVEMBER, SIX WEEKS MARRIED

You've asked me to tell you
what I want—for the world,

for myself, and for us:

I want to be the wound
and the linen that binds it,

the medicine that heals it,
the earth and the sky.

So come to bed.

It's late, and we're married now.

LOVE & BONE

If we are only bodies—
flesh and muscle, breath and bone,

temporary, fleeting,
motes of dust on a butterfly wing—

then let our time on earth
be a calendar of feasts:

days that bow, deep and shy,
as if to hide how fine they are;

and let the extravagant lace of evening
come and cover us like a veil—

we fortunate lovers,
                living our lives,
here, in our carnal kingdom.

REQUEST

You call out to us from the edge
of a field we sense but cannot see.

If you could, you'd get into a car,
set the gear, disappear into the night.

No one would question your leaving.
Your children are middle-aged now.

Here the pollen falls like dust
from the pines and great oaks.

It coats and shadows the glass
of the hospital windows.

Here, the Southern Bradford pear
hurls its blossoms into the world,

and the dogwood's thin branches
bear the weight of its own flowers.

You've made your life amid these woods.
Your children have settled elsewhere.

I come because you ask me to, bringing
my sister, your daughter, to see you.

You haven't seen her in years.
You speak to her in whispers.

She writes the names of the dead
on the backs of old Kodak prints.

I watch as the two of you work,
your hands making bridges

of spark and light and remembrance.

II. ASH

What do
they know, these
slim, dark forms,
still singed with crack-fire,
curving into their
church basement seats?

Later they will sleep—
bunked, bed-checked,
light as gas or ether,
while slivers of night
hang high above them,
lit by a cold North Star.

For now, they spill out
from transport vans,
and after the meeting
troop up to the podium,
billets in hand. I sign them,

every one, in the raw
unfiltered ink-black blood
of my own unfinished
disease.

SANDSTORM

The wind rises,

uproots trees,
darkens the sun,

swarms and browns
the evening air—

presses against me,
weakens and frees me,

lightens, lifts
the spirit from my body—

the body,
                pale grave.

JOE

Remember, Joe, those Saturday nights,
the year we were seventeen?

We'd take my father's El Camino,
glide forty miles
               of black-iced pavement
all the way into the city.

At Jim's Bar up on North Street,
we'd flash the bouncer our fake IDs

        and step straight into another world.

Free from judgment and prying eyes,
we'd lose ourselves
       in the smoke and sweat,
strangers' bodies pressed against our own—

we'd flirt and dance,
fall in love by the hour,

        two untouchable small-town boys

masquerading
as full-grown men.

        *

Hours later, past closing time,
we'd weave our way back
on familiar roads,

drinking Dewar's
straight from the bottle,
starlit, all the way home—

then silently turn
down the East Lake Road
to my family's cottage on Sandy Beach.

We'd shovel our way to the kitchen door,
the harsh lake wind
                cutting straight to the bone—

slip into the house,
        empty since summer,
head upstairs to my tiny room,

where, under dusty covers
on my fold-out bed
              we'd spoon,

until our frosted breath
faded
in the morning light.

*

At daybreak,
you'd quietly gather your things,

walk the two miles back to town
to tuck yourself
        into your own bed.

Unable to sleep, I'd make coffee,
carry a mug of it, steaming, out to the dock

where we'd languished all summer
the summer before,

dangling our legs
in the grey-green shallows,
inventing our California lives.

Of course, you were headed for San Francisco—
it was Los Angeles for me.

*

For how many years,
through how many loves
    had I told myself:

there would always be Joe,
the *Joe* I remembered—

  wild companion,
    breaker of rules—

until I heard
they'd found your body,
needle plunged in a tunnel of vein.

By the time I arrived at your rented room,
your belongings
were stacked outside the door.

In a pile of trash,
the rosewood box I'd given you
the year we both turned twenty.

*

A summer house on a winter lake.
The waning light of a slate-grey day.

I walk out onto frozen water,
the rosewood box in my hands.

Fifty feet out beyond the dock,
I rattle the hinges,
                pick at the latch—

then,
on a gust of gathering wind,

        a scatter
                of glittering ash.

PRAYER

When I was young
my prayer was brief, a plea:

> *Save me*

then, an endless
O of demand:

> *O give me*
> *everything*

Now I lie awake nights
listening for wolf-song

and send a new prayer
into great vaults
of sky:

> *Lord of all*
> *grant that I*
>
> *might be*
> *well used*

NEIGHBORHOOD WATCH

A faint call awakens me at six a.m., lifting up and over the greenbelt outside my bedroom window. It sounds like a lone desert bird, or maybe a homeless man calling out from the main road. The noise is muted but steady; it repeats every ten seconds or so, like the soft, insistent honking of a horn.

Then, a moment of recognition: my elderly next-door neighbor is calling out for help. His voice seeps through the concrete wall between our condominiums.

The body wants to live. It stakes its claim to the earth, states its intention to remain as long as possible. It will manage to report its distress, to reach out for assistance no matter the effort, no matter the cost.

*

The calls become louder as I approach his back door. From the backyard, I call his name, letting him know I'm on my way. Once he knows he has been heard, I can sense relief in his voice. I listen to him call out instructions: *There's a key in the birdcage. In a little blue box. Come in through the glass slider.*

I move through the dust and dirt of the cluttered back patio, past the abandoned birdcage. When I finally enter, he is lying face up, on the floor, in the hall, his cane thrown akimbo. A bowl of half-eaten plums on the kitchen counter, flies swarming over the rotting flesh of the fruit, ashtrays overflowing on the dining room table.

The air in the apartment is thick with the mingled smells of cat piss and stale cigarette smoke. A television blares in the bedroom. Looking up at me, my neighbor's face is bland and unlined as the face of a child. I kneel, take his hand. Twice before, he's greeted me when he's shuffled out to get his mail, and once, he waved from his worn-out patio glider. But I know, at that moment, to him I am a stranger.

Did you hit your head? I ask, and he mumbles something I can't understand. I slip a thin couch pillow under his head.

The body declares its intent to live. It claims its right to water, to air. The body calls out from the riverbed, from the floor of the volcano, the limb of the tree, from wherever it has been hurled or hung or left stranded and alone.

*

I've lived in this neighborhood for nearly four years. Until now, I've never heard his television, smelled his cigarette smoke, had any idea that a small, semi-feral cat lived right next door. Now, from the hallway, I see a flash of black dart under the bed.

My neighbor asks for water. I scan the room for a plastic bottle. *No, no*, he says, *the faucet, a glass*. I feel foolish and a little spoiled; I never drink water straight from the tap. *A straw*, he says, *I need a straw*, and points to the pantry.

I lift his head to the straw. The paramedics must be called—and my cell is at home on the bedside table. I find his phone with its large, square keys. Awkwardly, I place the call, and then, there is little more to be said and nothing to do except make him as comfortable as I can, offer some assurance through my touch.

But the truth is, I want to get out of there, to be rid of him, to simply be away. My skin is crawling, as if I'm covered with a film of dirt that I won't be able to wash off.

The body fights to live. It knows its own fragility as well as its resilience. It shuts down nonessential systems to preserve what is vital. In exigency, the body finds strength it could never otherwise muster.

*

Three paramedics enter, two diffident men and one efficient young woman. They administer their aid, ask the requisite questions of both me and my neighbor, and share their muttered assessments, just out of earshot. When they have loaded him safely into the ambulance, locked his front door, and driven slowly away, I stand outside and scan the neighborhood.

The body wants to live and go on living for as long as it can. If it survives the night, it strives to make some meaning of the morning. Listen, for it will declare itself—now singing a song in praise of life, notes ringing through the summer air; now moaning in pain like the winter wind whistling through a mountain pass. Now silent, simply holding on for its own dear life.

*

I close and lock the back-door slider, reenter the day through the open front door. I leave the kitchen chaos behind, the empty birdcage, some food for the cat.

The desert sun illuminates the late-spring morning. There's not a soul to be seen. Only the sparrows with their plain brown wings, and the crows, black marauders, pecking at trash by the side of the road.

ILLUMINÉ

When white fumes
first flared from shard

> *chalice of glass,*
> *illuminated—*

when the holy needle
first scraped the vein

> *Eros's dark blossom*
> *in a drop of blood—*

didn't you know
you were already bound?—

shackled to smoke-clouds,
chained at the bone.

THE JENKINS BOY

Someone prowls the common grounds,
looks in windows,
                scans for easy loot.

It's got to be the Jenkins boy:

tatted up, long-limbed,
hungry eye, sunken mouth—

he darts between rays
                of sand-stung light,
swerving, diving
like a vole in the moon-glow,

hiding in the bone-dry culverts,
drains that flowed
                deep and sweet with rain
before he landed here—

and now the fires, night after night.

How they crown the mountains,
leave soot in our hair.

                *

He takes pills, makes threats,
proclaims he was never loved—

        and all winter,
        pestilence blooms
        in the gardens, the fields—

the bloated clouds
    hold back their rain
until the groundwater turns brackish.

But still, no one hears the boy's complaints.

If only the profoundly wounded—
  the shuffling limb, the withered arm—
were as easily loved
as the brave and the beautiful.

*

Near the highest point of the range,
far above the trailhead,
just below the tree line,

he looks down to where the wind
has peeled away the palms' brown skins,

left them littered
    across the once-green lawns.

The things he'd wanted are all around him:

a blue transparency of sky,

the coming night
with its evening star,

the certainty
    of weightlessness.

DARKLING

Somewhere, a child is being beaten—

the sky loses an inch of light,
a star implodes,

a soul deflates
like a thin balloon.

Freud, the old father,
was right about these things:

If you are living,
you are brokenhearted.

Behind the veil,
the world is not benign.

*

Once, when I had been sleeping, soundly,

I suddenly sat upright,
felt my gut rise to my throat,

walked to the window,
pulled back the shade,

saw a great black wing
blot out the sky,

fly over and be gone.

I believe there are murderous men
hiding in plain sight

with their rifles and razors,
menacing words, hollow eyes.

And still, we parse the line
between sanity and evil,

intention and outcome, as if
knowing the cause of a violent act

might change the result
of its awful commission.

*

This morning, the light
lies low on the hills.

This morning, if God
is awake and watching,

the boy who yesterday
put a noose around his own neck

is sleeping, untroubled,
the next village over.

EASTER PORTRAIT, 1964 / (FATHER TO SON)

I hold the snapshot
close to the lamp.

The print is faded, sepia-toned;
only hints of color remain.

You were three years old,
and dressed for Easter—

shorts and knee socks,
sport coat, cap.

You are handing me a crocus.
I bend to receive it.

I am your father, twenty-five,
and you, my firstborn, eldest son.

Your grandmother's garden
is glazed with light.

*

I look up
from my hospital bed,

hoping for a glimpse
of Carolina moon.

My night-sky rider,
sweet bantling boy:

how far have you come
to make this vigil—

and what have I done
to deserve you so near.

MY FATHER'S DEATH

is grueling, slow.
It seems to take forever.

I watch his vanity slip away
as his hair turns
from auburn
        to the color of nothing,

the brilliantine a memory now.

As the doctors arrive
and the pouches and tubes
        are put in place,

as he reaches back in time
to charm the nurses,

his voice still honey-cadenced,
his flirtatious wink
        a beat too slow—

even now,
in his living room hospital bed

he is luminous,
completely surrounded by light.

        *

My father's death
has its own splendid agenda.

His timing is as exquisite
as when he was a horseman—

tracking the fractions,
                rounding turns,
saving ground for the long stretch run.

As he slowly lets go
                of his parcel of skin,
he asks the world's permission
to go on living awhile—

asks to be lifted and turned
toward the southern window,

for the gift of a sip of water,

for the grace
of an unassisted breath.

My father sleeps soundly
through the warm afternoons,

the world saying *yes*
to his every request.

                *

I dream that I take him home to die,
to the small row house he shares with his wife.

The two of them sit
                and talk, and talk—

about the dogwood,
how it's bloomed early this year,

and the sweet young filly that foaled last spring—

They walk together out to the barn.

My father wears his John Deere cap
and carries her heavy quilting bag.

I dream I see only the good in him.

THE FAMILY LINE
        —for Bridget

I've told the story so many times—

how I was exiled
from that wintry place,

pronounced dead by our parents,
cursed by our brother,

and you, at seven,
too young to be told the truth—

alone at a window,
waving goodbye
as they hustled me away.

        (There would be meadow grass,
         deep and fragrant; but that would not be
        for many seasons…)

        *

I found myself
in a second land of winter—

who could have known there was another North,
with bullwhip winds and cities built
with walkways in the air?

        (Even then, I believed
        I deserved the cold.)

I brushed aside
both sorrow and fear
with one swipe of the same gloved hand.

How to hope for summer
        when all you've known
is the pale green of an ice-coated lake,

the blue snow squall
that stings the eye—

        (*There would be seagrass and spindrift,*
         white-sand beaches lined with palm…)

      *

When the earth has flowered
and the veil has lifted

between you
and childhood's glimmering world—

    when you finally see
    that you, too, are wounded

and the drops of blood you shed
appear as rubies
        in the snow

then you'll know
I never intended
        to leave you.

Little sister,
you will know.

WHAT WAS PROMISED
                —after Cecilia Woloch

A scattering of roses,
a cut glass bowl.

The racing form,
some worthless tickets.

Luck, of my own making.

No homestead—
the land sold off,
the house demolished.

A wooden gavel,
passed down to the son
of a son of an auctioneer.

A clarion voice
like my father's voice
and my grandfather's voice.

A ring, yellow diamond,
given, then taken back.

Music, my first companion.

The brilliance of autumn,
ochre and orange-leaved days.

Mud-caked boots in winter.

And lakes, always a lake.

Snow.

MIGUEL

Tell me, Miguel:
           you, more human
and yet, more animal than I—

did you feel the need for solitude
so keenly that it became an ache?

In your nightly dreams
of the deep blue-green,

with your ear pressed against
the lips of the world,

did you hear what drove
those bitter waves,

that one long sigh
from the lungs of God?

A few missed breaths
and we pass from this world—

the night is falling
and falling fast.

Do you know, Miguelito,
how sharp the moon can be?

It can slice you
the way a knife slices an orange,

the way it carves me to pieces now
before your eyes—

eyes still open
long after you've abandoned this earth.

AFTERWORD

What I want you to know is that I did not survive. I want to tell you how the summer froze over, how I settled into the cottage, the one at the lake, told my family I had claimed it and would find a way to repay them later.

The snow fell in fragments. The old roan mare down on Poplar Beach didn't make it through the winter.

I want you to know that nothing happened to me all those years because I was not there, was not a person, did not exist. I was not anyone. My body endured, but I did not survive.

My father's rifle is there above the fireplace, your black parka on its hook by the door. Take them down; let's walk together. The ice is green and solid out beyond the pier.

ACKNOWLEDGMENTS

Thanks to the editors of these print and online journals in which these poems originally appeared, sometimes in slightly different versions or with different titles:

The American Journal of Poetry: "Coldwater Canyon Suite"

Cagibi: "'What do they know…'" (as "After the Meeting")

The Cape Rock: "Pinehurst, 2014 / (My Father to His Wife)"

The Comstock Review: "Afterword"

Crab Orchard Review: "Joe"

december: "Darkling"

The Greensboro Review: "Safe"

Mantis: "The Impossible Time"

Mudfish: "My Father's Death"

New Millennium Writings: "What Was Promised"

The New Guard: "The Jenkins Boy"

New Ohio Review: "'Didn't I stand there once…'" (as "Stopover on a Road Trip to L.A., 1981")

Poetry International: "The Gardener"

Poetry South: "Request" (as "Last Request"); "Easter Portrait, 1964 / (Father to Son)"

Passager: "Love & Bone"

Tupelo Quarterly: "Neighborhood Watch" (as "The Space Between Bodies")

Whistling Shade: "The Family Line" (as "For My Sister")

The Write Room: "Miguel"

"Time Travels of the Older American Poet" appeared in the anthology *Spectral Lines: Poems about Scientists*

(Alternating Current Press, 2019), edited by Leah Angstman. The poem is inspired by my great-grandfather Fred M. Locke (1861–1930), who was known as "The Father of the Porcelain Insulator."

Thanks to the editors of *Poetry International,* who selected "The Gardener" for the 2018 C.P. Cavafy Poetry Prize. "The Gardener" is for, and inspired by, my grandfather James L. Locke (1898–1969), and for Ismael.

"The Impossible Time" appeared in the online anthology *Older Queer Voices: The Intimacy of Survival* (2016–present), edited by Sarah Einstein and Sandra Gail Lambert.

"Coldwater Canyon Suite" and "The Impossible Time" appeared in the chapbook *Off Coldwater Canyon* (2021), published by The Poetry Box.

"Miguel" is inspired by Spanish poet, playwright, and social activist Miguel Hernández Gilabert (1910–1942), who died in prison, of tuberculosis.

GRATITUDE

Thanks to Lana Hechtman Ayers and her team at World Enough Writers for so lovingly shepherding this manuscript into the world.

Thanks to Cyrus Cassells and Sandra Alcosser for their lovely endorsements of this volume. And my deep appreciation to poet Mitchell Untch for the dedication of his poem "Rainsong" and for allowing a quote from the poem to be included in this book.

Thanks to acclaimed artist Salomon Huerta for providing his luminous artwork as the cover of this collection, and to George Jesús Meza for helping to facilitate it.

Thank you to my husband, Scott, who always provides love and support for my work. My gratitude and love to my late grandmother Alice Elizabeth Emerson, who first showed me unconditional love.

My deep appreciation to Cecilia Woloch, who mothered this manuscript into existence with patience and skill— thank you for so generously sharing your gifts.

Thanks, finally, to Lise Goett, poetry doula extraordinaire, who brought her warm, bright light to this project with kindness, wisdom, and grace. You made everything luminous again.

This book is dedicated to Daniel Nelms and to the innumerable men and women lost to HIV/AIDS.

ABOUT THE AUTHOR

C.W. Emerson's work has garnered numerous international accolades, including two awards from *Poetry International*: the C.P. Cavafy Poetry Prize (2018) and co-winner of the 2023–24 Summer Chapbook competition. Emerson's poetry and literary criticism have been featured in esteemed publications such as *Harvard Review*, *Oxford University Press*, *Greensboro Review*, *Tupelo Quarterly*, and more.

He is the author of *Danger Face* (Wayfarer Books, 2025), winner of the 2024 Homebound Publications Poetry Prize; a chapbook, *Off Coldwater Canyon* (The Poetry Box, 2021); and the prize-winning portfolio *The Thoracic Diaries*, forthcoming from *Poetry International*.

Emerson's poetry was a finalist for the Montreal International Poetry Prize (2020) and shortlisted for the International Beverly Prize for Literature (2019). His work has been anthologized in several poetry compilations containing themes relevant to the LGBTQIA+ communities.

Dr. Emerson is a retired clinical psychologist. He divides his time between Southern California and San Miguel de Allende, Mexico.

Visit his website at theolderamericanpoet.com.

www.ingramcontent.com/pod-product-compliance
Lightning Source LLC
Chambersburg PA
CBHW060538080526
44586CB00012B/793